ABOUT THE BANK STREET READY-TO-READ SERIES

More than seventy-five years of educational research, innovative teaching, and quality publishing have earned The Bank Street College of Education its reputation as America's most trusted name in early childhood education.

Because no two children are exactly alike in their development, the Bank Street Ready-to-Read series is written on three levels to accommodate the individual stages of reading readiness of children ages three through eight.

○ *Level 1:* GETTING READY TO READ (Pre-K–Grade 1)
Level 1 books are perfect for reading aloud with children who are getting ready to read or just starting to read words or phrases. These books feature large type, repetition, and simple sentences.

● *Level 2:* READING TOGETHER (Grades 1–3)
These books have slightly smaller type and longer sentences. They are ideal for children beginning to read by themselves who may need help.

○ *Level 3:* I CAN READ IT MYSELF (Grades 2–3)
These stories are just right for children who can read independently. They offer more complex and challenging stories and sentences.

All three levels of The Bank Street Ready-to-Read books make it easy to select the books most appropriate for your child's development and enable him or her to grow with the series step by step. The levels purposely overlap to reinforce skills and further encourage reading.

We feel that making reading fun is the single most important thing anyone can do to help children become good readers. We hope you will become part of Bank Street's long tradition of learning through sharing.

The Bank Street
College of Education

For Molly Elizabeth Davies
— W.H.H.

To my niece and nephew, Laura and David,
and Rocco the cat,
the dizziest dog I know
— G.B.

For a free color catalog describing Gareth Stevens' list of high-quality books and multimedia programs, call 1-800-542-2595 (USA) or 1-800-461-9120 (Canada). Gareth Stevens Publishing's Fax: (414) 225-0377.
See our catalog, too, on the World Wide Web: http://gsinc.com

Library of Congress Cataloging-in-Publication Data

Hooks, William H.
    A dozen dizzy dogs / by William H. Hooks; illustrated by Gary Baseman.
      p. cm. -- (Bank Street ready-to-read)
    Summary: A dozen dizzy dogs have an adventure with a bone.
    ISBN 0-8368-1748-6 (lib. bdg.)
    [1. Dogs--Fiction. 2. Stories in rhyme. 3. Counting.] I. Baseman, Gary, ill.
    II. Title. III. Series.
    PZ8.3.H765Do 1997
    [E]--dc21   97-1625

This edition first published in 1997 by
Gareth Stevens Publishing
1555 North RiverCenter Drive, Suite 201
Milwaukee, Wisconsin 53212 USA

© 1990 by Byron Preiss Visual Publications, Inc. Text © 1990 by Bank Street College of Education. Illustrations © 1990 by Gary Baseman and Byron Preiss Visual Publications, Inc.

Published by arrangement with Bantam Doubleday Dell Books for Young Readers, a division of Bantam Doubleday Dell Publishing Group, Inc., New York, New York. All rights reserved.

BANK STREET READY TO READ™ is a trademark of Bantam Doubleday Dell Books For Young Readers, a division of Bantam Doubleday Dell Publishing Group, Inc.

Printed in Mexico

1 2 3 4 5 6 7 8 9 01 00 99 98 97

Bank Street Ready-to-Read™

A Dozen Dizzy Dogs

by William H. Hooks
Illustrated by Gary Baseman

A Byron Preiss Book

Gareth Stevens Publishing
MILWAUKEE

ONE dizzy dog,
    digging all alone.

TWO dizzy dogs,
     digging up a bone.

THREE   dizzy dogs,
        scratching with their claws.

FOUR dizzy dogs,
pulling with their paws.

FIVE dizzy dogs,
loading up their prize.

SIX   dizzy dogs,
    flying through the skies.

SEVEN dizzy dogs,
    landing with a groan.

11

EIGHT dizzy dogs,
       picking up the bone.

NINE dizzy dogs, making a repair.

GLUE

TEN dizzy dogs,
    rushing to the fair.

ELEVEN dizzy dogs,
        entering their prize.

16

TWELVE dizzy dogs,
can't believe their eyes!

ELEVEN dizzy dogs,
singing, "Arf, we won!"

TEN dizzy dogs,
dancing in the sun.

21

NINE dizzy dogs,
      dividing up the bone.

EIGHT dizzy dogs,
        starting out for home.

SEVEN dizzy dogs,
riding on a train.

SIX dizzy dogs,
   running through the rain.

FIVE   dizzy dogs,
       swimming through a flood.

FOUR dizzy dogs,
     slipping in the mud.

THREE   dizzy dogs,
        racing to their homes.

29

TWO   dizzy dogs,
     hiding their big bones.

ONE dizzy dog,
    digging once again!

William H. Hooks is the author of many books for children, including the highly-acclaimed *Moss Gown* and, most recently, *The Three Little Pigs and the Fox*. He is also the Director of Publications at Bank Street College. As part of Bank Street's Media Group, he has been closely involved with such projects as the well-known Bank Street Readers and Discoveries: An Individualized Reading Program. Mr. Hooks lives with three cats in a Greenwich Village brownstone in New York City.

Gary Baseman is an award-winning illustrator whose work can be seen in *Time* magazine, *The Atlantic, Discover,* and *Sports Illustrated,* among other publications. He has also written and designed animation for television. Born and raised in Los Angeles, Mr. Baseman now calls Brooklyn, New York, home.